Preparing for
BAPTISM

Preparing for BAPTISM

A Personal Diary

Mez McConnell

10 Publishing
a division of 10 of those.com

Previously published in 2004 by Grace Publications Trust, 7 Arlington Way, London EC1R 1XA.

This edition first published in Great Britain in 2018

British Library Cataloguing in Publication Data
A record for this book is available from the British Library

ISBN: 978-1-912373-16-1

Designed and typeset by Pete Barnsley (CreativeHoot.com)

Printed in the UK

10Publishing, a division of 10ofthose.com
Unit C, Tomlinson Road, Leyland, PR25 2DY, England

Email: info@10ofthose.com
Website: www.10ofthose.com

Dedicated to Rev. Dr. Stephen Dray (OG)
who always believed in me

Contents

Part Four

Appendix

Preface

This little book is not intended to be an in-depth treatment on the subject of baptism. I am working on the assumption that the people using this material hold firm, biblical convictions about the ordinance of believer's baptism. Nor are any new or profound insights to be found within these pages. Indeed, I have drawn upon a wide variety of sources that I have, in effect, collated and adapted.

Most particularly I am indebted to the work of Victor Jack and his booklet, *Believe and Be Baptized* which was a great aid in completing Part Three.

This series of studies is basically meant as a practical aid to ministers, youth workers, and new believers. I have written it with the intention of it being used as a four part study course leading up to baptism.

Part One focuses on why you should be getting baptized in the first place and will, I hope, serve either as a timely reminder of what you may already know or as a help in clarifying your thinking about baptism.

Part Two gives you an opportunity to assess whether you are really ready to take the big step of getting baptized.

Part Three explains what it means to be baptized "into Christ" as well as covering some practical considerations. It offers some helpful hints on how to give a personal testimony when you are baptized (if that should be the practice in your particular church).

Part Four is probably the most important section of the book. It discusses how you as a believer are to persevere in the faith, and offers suggestions on how you can best resist the attacks of the devil. It also discusses the importance of Bible reading, quiet times, fellowship, communion, and public or corporate prayer. There is also a small section that suggests ways in which believers can overcome temptation.

Finally every section comes complete with seven days of quiet time reading notes connected to the whole theme of baptism. These are intended to both focus your mind and to encourage you to get into the habit of having a daily devotional.

Introduction

Next to becoming a Christian being baptized as a believer is one of the most important things that will happen to you. It is certainly not an optional extra to the Christian life but the next step in a life of obedience as you grow in the Christian faith. In some ways being baptized is like getting married.

1. You are making a public declaration of your love for the Lord Jesus Christ.

2. You are leaving your old way of life behind and pledging yourself to live your life for God rather than against God.

3. Your baptism says that you now have a new master the Lord Jesus Christ, and that you now belong to him completely. In a sense you are now spoken for, for in baptism he claims you as his own.

4. Your relationship to other people and the way you live your life will never be the same again.

What Baptism is

Chapter 29 of the Baptist Confession of Faith 1689 states:

1. Baptism is an ordinance of the New Testament, ordained by Jesus Christ, to be to the party baptized, a sign of his/her fellowship with him, in his death and resurrection; of him/her being engrafted into him (Rom. 6:3-5; Col. 2:12; Gal. 3:27); of remission of sins (Mk. 1:4; Acts 22:16); and of his/her giving up to God, through Jesus Christ, to live and walk in newness of life (Rom. 6:4).

2. Those who do actually profess repentance towards God, faith in, and obedience to, our Lord Jesus Christ, are the only proper subjects of this ordinance (Mk. 16:16; Acts 2:41; 8:36, 37; 18:8).

3. The outward element to be used in this ordinance is water, wherein the party is to be baptized, in the name of the Father, the Son, and of the Holy Spirit (Mt. 28:19-20; Acts 8:38).

4. Immersion, or dipping of the person in water, is necessary to the due administration of this ordinance (Mt. 3:16; Jn. 3:23).

Baptism is also a testimony of your own personal Christian experience. Indeed, it has often been described as "an outward, physical sign of an inward spiritual experience". It is a declaration of your own spiritual state. More importantly, it is a sign and a seal of God's grace in your life.

What Baptism is not

Baptism is not equivalent to salvation. Being baptized does not make you a Christian in and of itself. You become a Christian by being "born again" (Jn. 3:3).

Part One

Why Should We Bother Anyway?

Is baptism all that important? After all it cannot save us, so therefore we cannot lose our salvation by not being baptized. Just look at the thief on the cross in Luke 23:43. He didn't get baptized, so why should we?

Look up the following verses and complete the sentence in your own words.

1. Matthew 3:13; Luke 3:21

We should be baptized because ...

2. Matthew 28:19

We should be baptized because ...

3. Acts 2:38; 2:41; 8:12; 8:36; 10:48; 16:33

We should be baptized because ...

4. Matthew 3:6; Romans 6:4

We should be baptized because it is a sign of our ...

Note: Our sin is often described in Scripture as a "stain", so when we are forgiven for our sins it is often referred to as a "washing" (Is. 1:16-18; Acts 22:16).

5. Matthew 28:19

We should be baptized because it shows people that we are a ...

Note: Being baptized does not make you a member of the Baptist demomination, or of any denomination for that matter. It simply declares that you are a disciple/follower of the Lord Jesus Christ.

6. 2 Corinthians 5:17; Romans 6:4

We should be baptized because it marks the end of our

____________ self and the start of a ____________ and better life.

Note: More than this, baptism is our promise to live this new and better life on a daily basis. Martin Luther's *Small Catechism* states: "Baptism signifies that the old Adam in us is to be drowned by daily sorrow and repentance, and perish with all sins and evil lusts, and that the new man should daily come forth again and rise, who shall live before God in righteousness and purity forever."

7. 1 Corinthians 15:3-6

We should be baptized because we are making a personal statement of faith about the Lord Jesus Christ. These facts are:

1. That he ____________ for our sins according to the Scriptures (v. 3b).

2. That he was ______________, that he was ______________ on the third day according to the Scriptures (v. 4).

We know that these facts are true because the risen Lord Jesus Christ appeared to:

1. (v. 5a)

2. (v. 5b)

3. (v. 6a)

Summary

As we have seen there are a number of reasons why we should get baptized.

1. Baptism is a command given in the New Testament by the Lord Jesus Christ. Indeed, Jesus himself was baptized by John the Baptist in the River Jordan.

2. The early disciples of the Lord Jesus Christ taught and practiced baptism.

3. Being baptized indicates that not only are you a follower of Jesus but that you are committed to a life of obedience to God.

Note: When we step into the water to be baptized we are basically saying to people, "My life is not my own any more. It belongs to God". Stephen Gaukroger puts it like this: "Being a Christian involves obedience and loyalty. Giving your life to Christ is not a casual decision to be taken lightly; it's not just about having a nice feeling inside. When we become Christians we enlist in God's army: He becomes our supreme commander and we give up the right to run our own lives. He says, 'Be baptized', and so we must obey that order ... We may not like or understand the commander's orders, but if the army is to be effective in fighting the enemy, all the troops must obey Him."

For Personal Bible Study

DAY 1 Mark 1:1-8

Q: What two conditions did John lay down for those he began to baptize? (Compare Acts 20:21)

1.

2.

Something to think about:

1. Have you turned away from the sin in your life?
2. Have you put your faith and trust in Jesus Christ?
3. Are you wanting to live God's way now instead of your way? What evidence do you have of this?

DAY 2 Mark 1:9-13

Note: Jesus here shows his approval of baptism by asking John to baptize him.

Q: What was God the Father's response to the baptism of Jesus?

Q: What happened immediately after Christ's baptism?

Something to think about:

1. Why do you think Jesus was baptized?
2. Why do you think God was "well pleased" with Jesus after he had been baptized?
3. What is the main lesson we can take from this?
   Think of at least one way that you can apply that lesson to your life today.

DAY 3 Matthew 3:13-17

Note: Matthew looks at baptism from another perspective.

Q: Why did John not want to baptize Jesus?

Q: Why did Jesus not need to be baptized?

Q: Jesus is given a special title in this passage. What is it?

Something to think about:

Jesus was completely sinless, yet to fulfil the will of God he identified himself with the sinful human race. Write a small prayer to Christ thanking him for his love for you and renew your dedication to him once again.

DAY 4 Luke 3:21-22; John 1:32-34

Note: The word "Trinity" is never found in the Bible, although the concept of the "Trinity" is. The word "Trinity" means "tri-unity" or "three-in-oneness". The word is used to summarize the teaching found in Scripture that God is three Persons yet still one God.

Q: In addition to John who are the three persons mentioned in these verses of Scripture?

1.

2.

3.

Something to think about:

1. Can you pick out the three different Persons of the Trinity from Matthew 3:16-17?

2. God is "diverse" (three Persons) yet united (one God). Often in our church and/or youth group we have a diverse range of people who sometimes aren't united. How can you contribute in such a way as to help the members feel, and function as one body.

3. Pray for unity in the church and/or group you are involved with.

DAY 5 — John 3:1-8

Note: The same Greek word means both "wind" and "spirit".

Q: What one thing is even more important than baptism? (v. 3)

Q: Nicodemus came to see Jesus at night (Mt. 10:32-33) **so that he wouldn't be seen. Has there ever been a time when you've been embarrassed to admit in public that you're a Christian?**

Something to think about:

Begin to make a list of non-Christian friends and family whom you could invite to your baptism so that they can witness your public declaration of your faith in, and love for, the Lord Jesus Christ. Begin to pray for them and ask the Lord for opportunities to talk to them about your baptism.

DAY 6 — John 3:22-24; John 4:1-3

Note: One of the main ideas behind the concept of baptism is "washing" or "cleansing". In the Bible baptism is often linked with the ideas of cleansing and forgiveness (Mk. 1:4). Baptism expresses the washing away of a person's sins—like having a bath but with a deep spiritual significance!

Q: Why did John baptize in the River Jordan?

Q: Do you think that the amount of water was important? Why?

Something to think about:

1. Read John 3:30
2. Often when we give our testimony to people we try and make it sound exciting or we concentrate on the bad things that we have done in our lives. But what does this verse teach us about what the focus of our testimony should be?

DAY 7 — Matthew 28:16-20

Note: The evangelist Vance Havner once said, "Our Lord made discipleship hard and lost many prospective followers because He called them to a pilgrimage not a parade—to a fight, not to a frolic".

Q: After Jesus Christ's resurrection from the dead he gave his disciples three commandments.

What were they?

1.

2.

3.

Something to think about:

1. What do you think it means to "be a disciple" of the Lord Jesus Christ?

2. What do you think it means to "make a disciple" of the Lord Jesus Christ?

3. A disciple is never inactive in working for God.
   In what ways are you active for God?

Part Two

Am I Really Ready For Baptism?

We've looked at the biblical principles that explain why you should be baptized. Now, in the second part of our study, we turn our attention to ourselves. Are you really ready? If you are not, then you should know it by the end of this lesson.

What is true belief?

Before you can answer that you need to bear in mind three very important things:

1. **God hates sin. Read 1 John 1:5. God is holy, and pure, and good. And because God hates sin he must punish it.**

2. **The Bible also tells us something important about ourselves. Romans 3:23 tells us that we are:**

   (A)

   And Romans 6:23 tells us that the end result of our sin is:

   (B)

3. **The Bible also tells us something else about God. Romans 5:8 tells us:**

We have to recognize that we cannot save ourselves. Christ has done it all for us. All we can do is respond to God and we do that in two distinct ways.

First, there is a need for:

Repentance

Repentance is not just saying "sorry" or showing remorse for the bad things you have done in your life. Repentance is saying to God, "Yes I am sorry, and to prove it I am going to turn away from the things I used to think and do that have upset and offended you." True repentance happens when you turn away from your old life and promise to live a new life with God's help. When we become Christians our lives take on a new direction or, to change the picture, are turned upside down. God is not interested in your words unless they are backed up by your actions. God says he loves us. God showed he loves us by sending Christ to die on the cross. It is that action which gives meaning to the promises that he would come. So it should be with you. Your promise to lead a new life must be matched by action.

Secondly, there is a need for:

Faith

The facts of faith

Your faith must be in Jesus Christ and in him alone. Faith means taking Jesus at his word and accepting that he is the Son of the living God, fully God *and* fully man. It means accepting that when Christ was crucified at Calvary he bore your sins (and mine) in his body, taking the full punishment for them.

Read Mark 15:34

Because God is holy and cannot leave sin unpunished he turned his back on Jesus, his beloved Son. Jesus stood in the place of sinners and was separated from his heavenly Father.

We know that God accepted Jesus' sacrifice because he raised him from the grave on the third day. Not only that but faith means believing that in his power and love Jesus Christ is able and willing to save you now.

The early church fathers wrote down their beliefs in a sensible and orderly fashion. One example is known as "The Apostles' Creed" and is accepted by Bible believing Christians all over the world. So when we are talking about the facts of faith we are basically agreeing with them and believers who for two thousand years have confessed that:

I believe in God, the Father almighty, creator of heaven and earth.
I believe in Jesus Christ, His only Son, our Lord.
He was conceived by the power of the Holy Spirit
and born of the Virgin Mary.
He suffered under Pontius Pilate,
Was crucified, died and was buried.
He descended into hell.
On the third day He rose again.
He ascended into heaven,
And is seated at the right hand of the Father.
He will come again to judge the living and the dead.
I believe in the Holy Spirit,
The Holy universal church,
The communion of the saints,
The forgiveness of sins,
The resurrection of the body,
And the life everlasting.
Amen.

Personal faith

However, faith has to be much more than an agreement with a set of facts.

Read James 2:19

Your faith has to be genuine and personal. You must be able to say that you have a personal, daily relationship with Jesus Christ because you have trusted in him.

Read Romans 10:9

It is not enough that our parents are Christians or that we have been going to church since we were babies. That will not save us. If you are still not sure at this point it would be good to check off the points in the following list:

1. Have you recognized that you are a sinner, and that you need God's mercy in your life (Rom. 3:23)?

2. Have you turned your back on sin and everything you know that causes offense to God (Acts 2:38)?

3. Have you put your faith and trust in the Lord Jesus Christ for the forgiveness of your sins (1 Pet. 2:24)?

Important Point!

Read Luke 6:46

Is Jesus Christ Lord of your life right now, today? Are there areas in your life where he isn't Lord?

Read James 1:22

How do we know for sure?

When God is working in your life there are a number of signs that you can recognize that show that you have been truly converted. This is not a complete list but it gives a fair idea of what is going on in your life.

1. There is evidence of true repentance. You have turned from your old way of living and accepted a new way. For some of you that may mean not associating with people who could easily lead you astray. For others it may mean keeping out of the way of temptation. It could mean breaking off a relationship with a non-believer, or breaking off an adulterous relationship. It could mean a number of things, but it may well mean actually physically turning away from the things that you were doing before you put your faith in Jesus Christ and decided to follow him and his way (Mt. 16:24).

2. You have gained a new understanding of God's word which was never there before. And not only a new understanding but a new desire to read it regularly (1 Cor. 2:14).

3. You now feel that you belong not only to God but also to his people (1 Jn. 3:14).

4. You now have a new ability to pray and a desire to come before God and speak to him through prayer.

5. The things that used to tempt you and please you and give you enjoyment no longer hold the same attraction, because your focus has now changed from pleasing yourself to pleasing God.

6. Doubt comes creeping up on you in ways that you have never experienced before.

7. You have assurance from God through the indwelling of his Holy Spirit that you are now his child and that he is your heavenly Father (Rom. 8:16).

Summary

Read Matthew 3:8

What evidence did John the Baptist look for when he was baptizing?

Read Galatians 5:22-23

Paul told the Galatian Church, that true Christians could be identified by:

1.

2.

3.

4.

5.

6.

7.

8.

9.

Are you ready?

Use this time now to think and talk through any issues you may have become aware of. Are there any things in your life that you need to repent of before you move on to the next section?

For Personal Bible Study

DAY 1 Acts 2:37-42

Note: As Peter was preaching someone from the crowd interrupted him to ask a question.

Q: What was the question?

Q: What was the answer?

1.

2.

Q: If they did this they were told that they would receive two things. They were:

1.

2.

Day 1 continued ...

Q: What are the four things we are told that the people did immediately after they were baptized?

1.

2.

3.

4.

Something to think about:

Being a Christian is more than about being committed to Christ. It is also about being committed to his Word the Bible, and to his people. Are you committed to your local church? Are you committed to sitting under the teaching of the Word of God? Ask God to help you sort out little priorities in your life, and to help you to become more committed to him and to his people.

DAY 2 Acts 8:12-17

Note: The Jewish people hated the Samaritans, more so than ordinary Gentiles. They were a people of mixed race who were descended from Jews who had intermarried with the Assyrians after they had conquered the nation of Israel (2 Kgs. 17:24). John 4:9 underlines the hatred that Jews and Samaritans had for each other in Jesus' day.

Q: What four things happened to the Samaritans when Philip was preaching?

1. (v. 12a)
2. (v. 12b)
3. (v. 17a)
4. (v. 17b)

Something to think about:

Make sure in your mind that you are truly ready for baptism. For the early disciples getting baptized was a big step. In lots of cases it meant sure and certain death, and at the very least severe persecution. (Sadly, for many Christians around the world little has changed in this regard in the last two thousand years.) Sometimes people get baptized for the wrong reasons: because their friends are getting baptized or maybe because they like standing up in front of the church. It is an important step that you are taking so pray that God will continue to lead and guide you in your decision to be baptized.

DAY 3 — Acts 8:35-39

Note: The Ethiopian eunuch believes and is baptized.

Q: How did he come to know the Lord Jesus Christ?

1.

2.

Something to think about:

As the Ethiopian was traveling along the road with Philip they came across some water and the Ethiopian said: "Look here is water, why shouldn't I be baptized?" Think about how you came to know the Lord and think about how you stand today. Is there any reason why you shouldn't be baptized? Pray about any problems or sins that maybe hindering you spiritually at this time.

DAY 4 — Acts 9:17-19; 22:12-21

Note: Even though it does not in and of itself achieve our salvation, baptism is still a necessary ordinance. Paul was converted the moment he met Christ, and even though he turned out to be one of the greatest Apostles he was not exempt from baptism.

Q: What did Ananias say to Paul when he met him?

Q: What were the first two things that Paul did after this?

1.

2.

Something to think about:

Pray specifically for an unbelieving friend or family member. Pray for them as they come to your baptism and hear the good news about Jesus Christ.

DAY 5 Acts 10:44-48

Note: There is a very close connection between baptism and the Holy Spirit in the book of Acts.

Q: In this passage which comes first?

Q: Why were they baptized? (v. 48)

Something to think about:

Why are you getting baptized?
List your reasons and pray through them.

DAY 6 Acts 16:11-15

Note: It was not uncommon in New Testament times for whole households to come to faith in Jesus and to be baptized.

Q: What is the order again?

1. (v. 14)

2. (v. 15)

Something to think about:

It is very important for us as Christians to try and live a consistently godly life. Not only is such a life a good witness to outsiders but also to our families as well. Pray that God will continue to help you to live more like the Lord Jesus each day.

DAY 7 Acts 16:25-34

Note: The conversion of the Philippian jailor.

Q: What are the five stages of this story?

1. (v. 30) What question did the jailer ask Paul and Silas?

2. (v. 31) They replied ...

3. (v. 32) They spoke ...

4. (v. 33b) Immediately ...

5. (v. 34b) He was filled with ...

Something to think about:

In verse 32 we are told that Paul and Silas "spoke the word of the Lord" to the jailer. We do not know exactly what they told him about Jesus but we know that it was enough for him to believe and be baptized. How would you share your faith with a non-believer?

Part Three

Preparing For Your Big Day

How will I be baptized?

Christians from varying denominations baptise people in at least three different ways:

1. Sprinkling water upon the forehead.

2. Pouring water upon the head.

3. Immersion of the whole body in water.

What is important for us to remember is that whilst all the Christian denominations believe in the importance of baptism they differ as to how it is to be performed. We believe that the Bible teaches that the only fitting way to baptize a person is by complete immersion, unless there are severe physical or mental difficulties that would prevent this. In this event, your church leader should be happy to discuss possible alternatives. God knows what is in our hearts (1 Samuel 16:7) so each problem should be dealt with on its/their individual merit(s). However, we believe in baptism by complete immersion for the following reasons:

1. The word for "baptize" in the Bible (baptizo) literally means "to dip". The word was used by the Greeks to signify the dyeing of a garment or the drawing of water by dipping one vessel into another. In the Old Testament we read in 2 Kings 5:14 that Naaman dipped himself in the river Jordan seven times. In the New Testament the word is used in Luke 11:38 in the context of washing oneself.

2. When we come across baptisms in the Bible immersion is always the mode used. For example:

(A) Read Matthew 3:16. "As soon as Jesus was baptized he ...

(B) Read Mark 1:10. "As Jesus was coming ...

(C) Read John 3:23. Why did John the Baptist choose Aenon to baptize people? ...

(D) Read Acts 8:38-39. In verse 38 the Ethiopian went ______________________ into the water. In verse 39 he came ______________________ out of the water.

3. The teaching of Romans 6:3-6 gives us a very clear picture that baptism should be by immersion. In these verses we are told that baptism is a picture of death, burial, and resurrection.

(A) **DEATH**—Into the water. When we go down into the water we are recognizing that Jesus Christ died for our sins and that we as believers now die to our old sinful lives.

(B) **BURIAL**—Under the water. We see this very clearly in verse 4. Our baptism is in effect like a funeral for our old self. We are putting it to death and burial testifies this.

(C) **RESURRECTION**—Out of the water. Read verse 5. When we come up out of the water it will be to live a new life under the direct guidance of God.

It is for these reasons that we teach that immersion is the biblical way to be baptized.

So what?

Is it really that important how a person is baptized? The answer to that question is yes. When we became Christians we handed our lives over to Christ and over to the teaching of the Bible. One of the practical implications of this is that we now live under a new authority, the Bible. Its teachings guide us and lead us in the way we should live our lives. To the best of our ability, we should seek to follow the commands and lessons that it has for each of us. As we have seen there is a biblical pattern for baptism, so we should seek to follow it as closely as possible. Jesus Christ himself spoke these words in John 14:15: "If you love me, you will obey what I command."

Sharing your faith

This is the integral part of your day. At some point during the service (you will be informed in advance) you may be asked to get up and share your faith-experience with everyone there. In Christian circles this is often called sharing your testimony.

Testimony? What and why?

> *Always be prepared to give an answer to everyone who asks you to give the reason for the hope that you have. (1 Pet. 3:15)*

The Greek word "marturion", from which we get the English word "martyr", is usually translated as "testimony". The word means, "saying by word and/or action to others something about what has been going on in a person's life." Whilst baptism itself is a kind of testimony in action, you will need to explain yourself very clearly to those present who may not be fully aware of the way that God has been working within you. Sharing a testimony gives you a remarkable opportunity to share the good news about Jesus Christ with those who have never heard and may never hear again.

It is vitally important that you realize and understand that your testimony must not be vague. It is not a good idea to say things like, "I gave my life to God" because whilst that may be true, to non-believers that could mean any number of so-called modern day "gods". Your testimony, then, should center on, and point to, the person and work of the Lord Jesus Christ. When Christ spoke in Acts 1:8 he told his followers that they should be witnesses to him. When you give your testimony you are not simply telling a nice story: you are proclaiming the good news about the Lord Jesus Christ.

An outline of a testimony

A good testimony will consist of three parts:

1. Before you became a Christian

(A) Describe your upbringing. Was it religious or not?

(B) What was your attitude towards Jesus Christ, Christianity and the church in general?

(C) What was your lifestyle like?

2. At the time of your conversion

(A) Describe how you became aware of what "sin" against God means and of your need to be saved (Rom. 3:23; 6:23).

(B) Explain how the implications of Christ suffering and dying on the cross became personal to you (Rom. 5:8; 1 Cor. 15:1-5).

(C) Tell how you came to realize that the only way to a restored relationship with God is through Christ.

(D) Explain the circumstances under which you asked Jesus Christ into your life as your personal Lord and Savior.

3. After your conversion

(A) What specific changes are obvious in your attitude and lifestyle (2 Cor. 5:17; Gal. 5:22-23)?

(B) In what specific way(s) are you now serving, or hope to serve, the Lord Jesus Christ (Rom. 12:3-8; 1 Cor. 12:11-27)?

(C) What is the basis for the assurance you have of your salvation (Rom. 8:16)?

(D) Why are you being baptized (Acts 2:38)?

Some tips for sharing your testimony

A carefully prepared short testimony can be of immediate and effective use in any witnessing situation. A good testimony holds attention and clarifies truth by illustrating it and making it personal and easy to understand. Personal experience always communicates well.

Preparing your testimony

1. First and foremost pray for wisdom and clarity, and pray for those who will listen.

2. Write it out in three simple paragraphs on a separate sheet of paper under the headings: before, during, and after.

3. Be concise. Cut out all unnecessary words and phrases. Be enthusiastic and recognize that God has frequently used a "very ordinary testimony" to speak to an individual. Be specific. Make clear, definite statements. Don't try to be funny and don't try to be clever.

4. Be specific when talking about how you came to know Christ. This helps those who are listening, in the event that they themselves want to follow your example and become a follower of Jesus Christ.

5. Emphasize the difference that being a Christian has made to your life: changed attitudes, morals, living, etc. Talk about the benefits of being a Christian: hope, love, peace, etc.

6. Emphasize the person and work of the Lord Jesus Christ.

7. Where possible try and share the full gospel message in your testimony. Speak of Christ's death for your sins and his resurrection to be your Lord.

8. When you are speaking try to look at people. Speak slowly and clearly and don't mumble. Use pauses and variations in emphasis, tone, and volume. Avoid nervous mannerisms. Smile—take a deep breath and begin. If you find the congregation too scary to look at then fix your eyes on a point somewhere on the horizon. This gives the impression

that you are looking straight at them. In order to minimize nervousness practice your testimony through several times. Time yourself. You should be between 5-10 minutes long. Cut bits out if it is longer and do not worry too much if it is shorter. A man called Robert Belton said: "As long as our testimony exalts the glory of Christ as Savior rather than our character either before or after conversion, it will be helpful."

9. Be positive—but do also be honest. If you have had no problems since you became a Christian, feel free to say so. On the other hand, if you are as normal as the rest of us (and you do encounter problems), feel free to admit that as well!

10. Have a definite, planned conclusion.

Dangers to look out for

1. Do not in any way try and glamorize your sinful lifestyle before you became a Christian. Do not give any glory to Satan but make sure you focus on Christ at all times. John Hunter once said, "God did not save you to be a sensation. He saved you to be a servant."

2. Try, where possible, not to use Christian jargon. Most ordinary non-Christian people (particularly those who have never attended a church and/or a Christian service before) often do not understand what we mean when we use the words "saved", "convicted", "converted", "sin". Remember that phrases commonly used by evangelicals are frequently misunderstood, and this would include "born again" and even the word "Christian". However, very often you cannot help using these

words, so when you do, try to remember to explain simply and clearly what they mean.

3. Don't criticize or attack other Christians, churches or denominations even if you've had a negative experience.

Remember, remember, remember

Remember that most of the people out there are on your side and they will be silently praying for you. They are interested in what you are saying and many of them will have been praying for you for many months and even years. Remember the words of Philippians 4:13: "I can do everything through him who gives me strength."

Practical advice and questions

Your church leader should talk you through what will happen at the baptismal service, but here are some questions you may like to ask and some advice to consider.

1. Do you need to choose a song or Bible passage that has a special significance for you? Can they be included in the baptismal service?

2. What will you be wearing to be baptized? Do you wear your own clothes or something that's provided for you? If you're wearing your own clothes, make sure that what you wear is not see-through because your clothes will cling to you when they get wet. It might be a good idea for ladies to wear a swimming costume under their clothes. Don't forget to bring a complete change of clothes with you on the day. You may also need a towel and a plastic bag for your wet garments.

3. What time should you arrive at the church before the service? Will there be a prayer time?

4. Should you have someone sit with you, a friend or relative who can look after your shoes, jewelry, phone, towel, etc.

5. You need to know that no one has ever drowned whilst being baptized. So, if you're nervous on the day (and you will be) just take a deep breath before you are lowered backward into the water. Please remember to keep your legs straight on the way down and to bend your knees on the way up. Try and remain as relaxed as possible.

For Personal Bible Study

DAY 1 Acts 18:8-11

Note: The book of Acts gives us a comprehensive and accurate account of the life and ministry of the apostle Paul. It is a hugely important document because it charts the first few decades of the Christian church.

Q: What did Paul preach about when he was in Corinth?
(1 Cor. 2:2)

Q: What do we learn about Crispus from this passage of Scripture?

1.

2.

3.

Q: What happened to Paul in Corinth?

Q: What did God say to Paul?

Something to think about:

Paul suffered a great deal of mocking and persecution for spreading the Christian message and it would have been very easy for him to give up. Sometimes opposition to the message can get us down but we need to listen to the words of verse 9. Pray for strength in your walk with the Lord.

Day 2 — Acts 19:1-7

Note: 12 men were baptized into the name of Jesus. Notice that they heard and believed before they were baptized.

Q: What is the difference between the baptism of John the Baptist and the baptism of Jesus?

1. John's baptism was a sign of ________________________ .

2. Jesus' baptism was a sign of ________________________ .

Something to think about:

Baptism in and of itself does not give us some sort of supernatural power to defeat the sin in our lives. We must keep on battling with the sin in our lives remembering what our baptism commits us to (Rom. 6:8-13). Pray for the help of the Holy Spirit to live as Christ would want you to.

DAY 3 Galatians 3:23-29

Note: Faith, baptism, and fellowship are all very closely connected.

Q: How do we get right with God?

(v. 24) We are justified by ______________________________ .

Q: What is the purpose of the law (v. 24)?

Q: What does faith in Christ remove (v. 28)?

Something to think about:

Baptism offers us an opportunity to confess our faith publicly. In the New Testament baptism and faith go hand in hand. Baptism then and now marks the beginning of our life within the Christian community. Start thinking about the prospect of church membership. Pray for your local community of believers and pray too that you will play an active role in the local church.

DAY 4 1 Corinthians 1:12-17; 6:11

Note: Baptism means that we are now under the exclusive ownership of Jesus Christ.

Q: What was Paul's main task?

Q: How could the cross of Christ be emptied of its power?

Something to think about:

Consider what is being said in verse 18. Only prayer can open the unbelieving minds and hearts of our friends and family. Continue to pray for those whom you have invited to witness your baptism.

DAY 5 1 Corinthians 10:1-5; Hebrews 11:6

Note: The crossing of the Red Sea offers us a picture of baptism.

Q: Does everyone who is baptized go to heaven?

Q: Why not?

Something to think about:

Baptism in and of itself cannot and does not save us. Our faith must be rooted in Christ. True faith then produces fruit that shows itself in a life of obedience to God. He has bought us and he now owns us. Pray for faithfulness and ask him to help you in the weak areas of your life.

DAY 6 — 1 Corinthians 12:12-14; 15:29

Note: Paul in 15:29 is not recommending that we get baptized for our dead relatives. He is merely pointing out that if there is no resurrection from the dead then those who used to practice this in the first century are very foolish.

Q: How does Paul describe a true Christian?

(v. 13) Baptized into ______________________________ .

Q: What differences between Christians does Paul point out in 12:4-7?

Something to think about:

When we become Christians God gives us a gift or gifts that are to be used to help the church and our fellow Christians. Pray to God asking him to show what specific gift (or gifts) he has given you and how you can put it to its best use.

DAY 7 — Romans 6:1-4

Note: Baptism signifies union by faith with the Lord Jesus Christ.

Q: What four things are illustrated in the service of believer's baptism?

1.

2.

3.

4.

Something to think about:

Being baptized signifies that we are making a complete break with our old way of life and sin. Once we make that public declaration people (particularly non-Christians) will be watching us closely to see if we stumble and fall. Pray that you will remain as consistent as possible in your Christian walk and so be a good ambassador for the Lord Jesus Christ.

Part Four

Running The Race

> *Therefore, since we are surrounded by such a great cloud of witnesses, let us throw off everything that hinders and the sin that so easily entangles, and let us run with perseverance the race marked out for us. Let us fix our eyes upon Jesus, the author and Perfecter of our faith, who for the joy set before him endured the cross, scorning its shame, and sat down at the right hand of the throne of God. (Heb. 12:1-2).*

Much has been written about how Christians should cope with the spiritual attacks that often follow baptism (and indeed plague Christians throughout their earthly lives). It is not unusual for believers to experience a real period of attack by the devil after their baptism, not unlike that faced by Jesus in the wilderness after his own baptism (Mt. 4:1-11). We must be clear that these temptations were unique to Jesus yet they do offer us an insight into the way the devil works.

We are warned in Scripture that the devil "prowls around like a roaring lion seeking someone to devour" (1 Pet. 5:8). Therefore, we are to always be on our guard. Paul in his letter to the Ephesians told the believers there to put on the full armour of God as we battle against the spiritual forces of evil (Eph 6:10).

It is wise, therefore, to be prepared to expect trials and troubles in our walk with Christ. We have an enemy who will seek to discredit us and our witness at every opportunity. He cannot take away our salvation for that has been secured by Christ for eternity (Jn. 10:28) but he can attack our faith and our confidence in God. During the baptismal stage of our Christian life this danger seems to be intensified for a number of reasons:

1. Very often our baptismal service can leave us with a real spiritual "high" for weeks after the event. You have publicly declared your love for, and your obedience to, the Lord Jesus Christ. The

devil is not happy with this and he will seek to destroy your joy and undermine your confidence in Christ.

2. Because of the emotional "high" of the day you may get the idea that from now on the Christian life is always going to be this exciting. In reality, this is not always the case. After the initial excitement has worn off we find ourselves back into the normal daily routine of Christian living. Somebody once said that the Christian life is "drill as well as thrill".

Enemy attack

Stephen Gaukroger has helpfully pinpointed several ways in which Christians can come under satanic attack, particularly following their baptism. They include:

Disillusionment or despair

It is easy to feel a sense of "anti-climax" after your baptism is over because of the intensity of preparing for, and praying about, the whole day. The feeling of God being right there with us, sometimes almost tangibly, often doesn't last. Sometimes we don't feel any real emotion at all and as we try and look back on the event it can all seem a bit of a blur. This can lead to feelings of disillusionment and despair which the devil can use to try to disturb your relationship with God.

Isolation

One of Satan's favourite schemes is to try to convince Christians that we're on our own and that nobody really understands us and how we are feeling. He will use anyone, including our family and friends, to try to make us believe us that our baptism was just a big hoax, a "phase" we're going through. But that is a lie. God made a promise to Joshua, many thousands of years ago when he told him: "Never will I leave you and never will I forsake you" (Josh 1:5). That promise still remains for all Christians today. In fact, we need never be alone again. Because of Christ's atoning death, Hebrews 10:22 informs us that all confessing sinners can now "draw near to God". Satan may attack us but if we continue to walk with Christ he can never isolate us from our heavenly Father.

Rejection

This is a key area in Satan's schemes against believers. If we feel disillusioned and/or isolated we can often transfer these emotions to fellow Christians. We may think that they don't actually care about us and our problems, but they really do! No problem is too small and unimportant. If you are suffering from any of these feelings then tell someone immediately. Talk to a friend or a confidant and ask them to pray for you. Things always look different after prayer. Scripture teaches us to "lift up holy hands in prayer" (1 Tim. 2:8) and to "pray in the spirit on all occasions with all kinds of prayers and requests" (Eph. 6:18).

Running the race

Problems, doubts, fears, and temptations are not just passing phases in the Christian life. Becoming a Christian will not guarantee anyone a problem free life. In fact the Scriptures clearly indicate just the opposite. Jesus said in Matthew 10:38, " ... anyone who does not take up his cross and follow me is not worthy of me." In biblical times the cross was the ultimate object of shame. It was reserved for the lowest kind of people: murderers, robbers, and all types of criminals. In effect Jesus is saying that if we want to follow him we must endure the scorn and humiliation of the world. Paul, in writing to the Philippians, tells them, " ... it has been granted to you on behalf of Christ not only to believe on him, but also to suffer for him" (Phil 1:29).

Read 1 Corinthians 9:24-27

If we are to survive the attacks of Satan and continue on in the Christian faith then we have to be realistic. We have to take a long term view. In effect, Paul is teaching the Corinthians in these verses that the Christian life is not a 100 meters sprint. It is more like a marathon. Being baptized, then, means that we've only just left the starting line. If you've ever watched a marathon you will know that it is a very gruelling event. Such is its difficulty that it is very rare for all of the original runners to complete the race. Many pull out with injuries, some give up through sheer exhaustion, some only go on for a little while and a few make it all the way to the finishing line. The same applies to the Christian life. In fact one word sums up what the Christian life is all about.

Read Hebrews 12:1

Perseverance is the key to the Christian life. Persevering in the face of all life's problems and Satan's attacks. It is God's will that we persevere in times of suffering because it is God's means for building character for his children. "We know," said Paul to the Romans, " ... that suffering produces perseverance; perseverance, character; and character hope" (Rom. 5:3-4). But, like all good athletes, we need to develop a training program to help us in the great spiritual race. We need to be disciplined if we are to persevere in the faith. Christians have the perfect training manual, the Bible, to aid us in this goal.

Developing a training program

Read Acts 2:41-42

In verse 42 we find four disciplines that the early Christians devoted themselves to in order that they might stand firm in the faith.

1. The Apostles' teaching

In plain words, we need to be reading the Bible on a regular basis. Without this discipline Christians can never hope to gain strength. If we are to grow in faith and understanding then we need to be spending time, where possible, reading, studying, and meditating on the word of God. It would be helpful to develop the discipline of setting aside some time each day to devote ourselves to this practice. In evangelical circles this is often known as having a quiet time. Now we must be clear that there is no direct command found anywhere in Scripture that instructs us to have a quiet time. Devotion to the apostles' teaching in this context is not a reference to reading the Bible, firstly because the Scriptures as we have them today had not been systematically formulated yet and, secondly, because many of the early church were illiterate and so would not have been able to read the Bible had it been available to them.

However, our New Testament contains not only the teachings of Christ but the Apostles' teachings also and therefore we would do well to devote ourselves to the understanding of them. The practice of a regular quiet time is important because through this discipline we grow in grace and in the knowledge of our Lord and Savior. More than that, says Paul, our Bible is the "sword of the spirit" (Eph. 6:17) and is a powerful weapon against the devices of Satan.

Having a quiet time

When and where we take time out to spend praying, praising, and reading God's word is purely a matter of personal preference. Here are some suggestions:

1. Find a quiet place, if this is possible, where you won't be disturbed. It is much easier to focus on God without the countless distractions of those around us.

2. Be flexible in your approach to your quiet time. If you have access to one, read a devotional book or a study book. You could read the Bible in chapters or follow a year long reading program. Find the method that bests suits you. There is no standard way to read the Scriptures—just as long as you're doing it!

3. Some people prefer to have some Christian music on in the background as an aid to worship and prayer.

4. As part of your quiet time you could read a chapter of a good book. Testimony type books are often very encouraging, or if you're feeling very adventurous Bruce Milne's *Know The Truth* is an excellent tool to familiarize yourself with the basic beliefs of the Christian faith. (Milne, Bruce, *Know The Truth* (IVP, 2014).

5. Make a prayer list of family, friends, missionaries, church members, and any others. Pray for them altogether or on different days of the week. For example, have a day just focusing on missionaries, another for unbelievers, etc. Using one of the Psalms as a basis for writing a personal prayer to God is another good discipline. Be imaginative when it comes to prayer.

6. If you are beginning to feel bored by your routine then change it! It is often very difficult to be disciplined in your quiet time so it is not unusual to find that they can be hard work. Continue to persevere even through the dry times.

7. Always pray before you open your Bible. Psalm 119:18 offers us a good start: "Open my eyes that I may see wonderful things in your law."

8. Don't panic if you miss a day or two in your weekly routine. We have a loving and forgiving God. He understands when we fail to achieve our aim of a daily quiet time. Many believers throughout history have hit dry times when they have felt spiritually far from God. Take encouragement from the fact that God's love for us and, more importantly, our salvation, do not hinge on our performance of religious rituals. However, God does expect us to live disciplined lives so we need to get back in to our routine as soon as possible.

2. Fellowship

Fellowship comes from the Greek word, koinonia, and means to share in or to participate in something at an intimate level. The book of Acts records that fellowship was an important factor in the life of the early church.

Read Acts 2:44-47

Scripture teaches us that when we become Christians we enter into fellowship with God the Father through the Lord Jesus Christ. We can now relate intimately to God through prayer, Bible reading and study (in our modern context) and the singing of hymns, psalms, and spiritual songs.

Fellowship also has a human dimension in that once we become disciples of Jesus Christ we enter into membership of his worldwide church. This means that Christians from every corner of the planet can enjoy fellowship together, united by the same faith in Jesus Christ. At a local level it is advisable to join a local worshipping community as soon as possible. Some people prefer not to commit themselves to membership of a local church or fellowship but there is a big difference between merely attending a church or fellowship and becoming a full member.

There are many benefits and privileges to being a member of your local worshipping community:

1. The feeling of belonging and being cared for.

2. Being prayed for.

3. Opportunities to serve God.

4. Being involved in decision-making processes.

5. Being encouraged in your walk with God and, when necessary, being disciplined.

Alongside the benefits are the responsibilities:

1. We need to be meeting with other Christians on a regular basis (Heb. 10:24-25).

2. We have a responsibility to pray for other believers (Mt. 18:19).

3. We have a responsibility to use our God given gifts for his glory and for the benefit of our local worshipping community (Eph. 4:16; 1 Cor. 12).

4. We need to be giving our time, money, and possessions as God directs us.

5. We need to maintain a consistent Christian witness by living a holy, God honoring life, accountable to local leadership (1 Cor. 5:9; Eph. 2:21).

6. We have a responsibility to welcome others to the local Christian community, demonstrating to them the love of Christ in word and deed.

Thus, the concept of fellowship is of fundamental importance to all Christians. The Christian life is not meant to be a solitary life. It is God's intention for believers to grow and mature in the faith surrounded by likeminded people. Because of this, Satan will try and keep you from regularly attending services and other times of fellowship. It is important that we recognize the danger signs very early on. Our local church or fellowship may not be everything we want it to be but, nevertheless, we are still obligated to attend and play a part in its life.

3. The breaking of bread

In Christian circles this is often referred to as "The Lord's Supper" or "Communion". These three terms can be used interchangeably. The breaking of bread is known as the second ordinance given by Christ to the church (the first being baptism itself). Not only did the Lord Jesus institute this ordinance but he commanded his followers to continue to observe it throughout their earthly lives or until his return.

The breaking of bread and the drinking of the cup are symbols of Christ's broken body and shed blood for guilty sinners. Thus, the breaking of bread is important because it gives Christians an opportunity, at regular intervals, to remember the Lord Jesus Christ and his sacrificial death on their behalf. Not only that, it is also a clear sign of the unity of God's people as they come together to remember him.

4. Prayer

Early, bitterly persecuted, African converts to Christianity on the island of Madagascar used to be very earnest and regular in their private devotions to God. Each one reportedly had a secret spot in the forest where he or she would retreat to in order to meet with God in prayer. Over a period of time, and because of extensive use, these paths would become well worn. As a result, if any of the believers began to neglect their prayer life, it was soon apparent to the others. They would kindly remind the negligent one: "Brother, the grass grows on your path."

Prayer is another key part of the Christian life. It has many aspects. Prayers can be made to God for ourselves (known as petitions) or on behalf of others (known as intercession). Prayer can consist of confessions of sin, adoration, praise, and thanksgiving to God.

Although prayer may have many aspects, the Bible teaches us that there are only two kinds of prayer: private or personal and public or corporate.

Private or personal prayer

Private prayer is important because it was taught by Christ. "When you pray, go into your room and pray to your Father, who is unseen" (Mt. 6:6). Jesus was speaking in this text against the hypocrisy of the Pharisees who loved to show their piety by praying publicly on street corners. Even Jesus used to spend time alone in private prayer with his heavenly Father.

In Luke's Gospel we read that the disciples asked the Lord Jesus to teach them how to pray (Lk. 11:1-12). Jesus, in response to their request, proceeded to teach them what has historically been referred to as, "The Lord's Prayer". This prayer offers believers a model to follow in their own devotional life. However, it is important to note that there are no explicit guidelines set down in Scripture for how we are to pray. Some of the most powerful prayers are the most simple. God is less interested in the form of our prayers than he is in the attitude of our hearts. That said, approaching God in prayer is to be done with the reverence befitting to his glory and majesty.

One popular and extremely simple model of prayer is known by the acronym, ACTS. This model is based loosely on the Lord's Prayer.

Adoration

Start your prayer time by praising the Lord for who he is, for his goodness to us, for his creation, etc. Sometimes it is helpful to begin by reading a Psalm of praise. If you have access to the material, the words to a hymn, song or chorus can also serve as a starting point to express your adoration to God.

Confession

It is always good to confess our sins before our heavenly Father. In "The Lords Prayer" Jesus says that we are to ask God to, "forgive us our sins". If there is a particular sin you are struggling with in your life it is good to bring it to God.

Thanksgiving

Thanksgiving is an important part of our prayer life. The Apostle Paul, speaking to the Colossian Christians, urged them to "be thankful" (Col. 4:2). He also encouraged the church in Thessalonica to "give thanks to God in all circumstances" (1 Thes. 5:18). For what are we to give thanks? Many Scriptures urge us to be thankful to God for his grace and provision to us in our lives (1 Chr. 16:8; Ps. 100:4; 107:1; Phil. 4:6).

2 Thessalonians 1:1-12 offers us an insight into the prayers of the Apostle Paul. Believers should do more than just give thanks for their own lives. In this heartfelt passage of Scripture we read of Paul's prayer for his brothers and sisters. He is thankful for their growing faith and

for their love for one another in verse 3. In verse 4 he informs them that he is thankful for their perseverance in the faith despite severe trials and hardships. Our prayers of thanksgiving should always mention our fellow believers.

Supplication

Pray for your friends and family on a regular basis. If possible it is good to make up a prayer diary and pray for particular people on certain days of the week. Often in the Christian life issues come up at certain times. We hear of believers being persecuted or of someone in specific need. During these times we need to pray earnestly as the early church did for the release of Peter from prison (Acts 12:5, 12-16). This type of praying often involves perseverance because it may occur over a long period of time. Luke tells us that Christ often withdrew to pray and once he even prayed all night long (Lk. 5:16; 6:12). Paul encourages the Ephesian believers to "pray in the spirit on all occasions with all kinds of prayers and requests ... always keep on praying for all the saints" (Eph. 6:18).

Public prayer

Believers can find great strength and comfort in praying together. Jesus assumes that believers would pray together when he talks to his disciples about church discipline in Matthew 18:15-20. "Where two or three are gathered together in my name, there am I with them" (Mt. 18:20). Public prayer is a discipline that will only serve to strengthen God's church.

Summary

This, then, is the battle plan for running the Christian race well: studying the Word of God; fellowship; communion; prayer.

Not only will these disciplines equip you to deal with your baptism day but they will also serve you well throughout your Christian pilgrimage. There are those who started the Christian life well but, over time, fell away at some point (2 Tim. 4:10). In order to avoid this in our own lives we need to be disciplined and we need to persevere even in difficult times. We must make it our aim to be like the apostle Paul who, looking back over a difficult life, was able to boldly declare: "I have fought the good fight, I have finished the race, I have kept the faith" (2 Tim. 4:6).

For Personal Bible Study

Day 1 Romans 10:9-13

Note: Baptism is an acknowledgement of the complete lordship of the Lord Jesus Christ over our lives. We are saying that he has total authority over every area of our lives.

Q: What two things in verse 9 does Paul teach are necessary for salvation?

1.

2.

Something to think about:

Is Jesus Christ really the Lord of your life? Can you think of any area in your life where Christ is not Lord? Pray about it and ask the Holy Spirit to help you submit your whole life to the Lord.

Day 2 Colossians 2:11-15

Note: Again, it is important to remember that being baptized is not a magical ticket into heaven; it is a sign that you have been "born again".

Q: According to verse 12 baptism symbolizes at least two things. What are they?

1.

2.

Something to think about:

How will you respond to non-Christian friends or family who ask you to explain the significance of your baptism?

Day 3 — 1 Timothy 6:12; Titus 3:4-7

Note: Baptism marks the beginning of a new chapter in your Christian life. You have confessed publicly that Jesus Christ is your personal Lord and Savior, and now the battle begins.

Q: How does Paul describe the Christian life? (1 Tim. 6:12)

Q: What is the primary cause of our salvation? (Tit. 3:5)

Something to think about:

1. Have you realized the full extent of what God has saved you from? Think about it for a moment. Offer up a prayer of thanks that God in his mercy has saved your soul.
2. Do you realize the full extent of the battle that you have been saved to fight? Think about that also. Pray for strength to persevere when the going gets tough in your Christian life.

Day 4 Ephesians 5:24-27

Note: In this passage of Scripture Paul is dealing with the love a husband is to have for his wife. A husband's love should follow the example of the true love that Christ has for his church. Christ loved her so much that he gave up his own life for her.

Q: How is the believer made clean from the stain of sin in their life? (v. 26)

Q: What does God desire from you as a believer? (v. 24)

Something to think about:

How can you make sure that you are walking in obedience to God? Are you having a regular quiet time for reading and prayer? You need to do this if you are to grow in your faith.

Day 5 — Hebrews 6:1-2; 10:19-25

Note: The letter to the Hebrews was written to a group of Christians who were under intense pressure to give up their faith.

Q: What are the six elementary teachings found in the first two verses of Hebrews chapter 6?

1.

2.

3.

4.

5.

6.

Q: Now turn to chapter 10. What two facts is the writer concerned with in the passage?

1.

2.

Day 5 continued ...

Q: What three things are we urged to do in this passage?

1. (v. 22)

2. (v. 25)

3. (v. 25)

Something to think about:

1. How do we "draw near to God"?

2. How do we make sure that we continue to grow in maturity in our faith?

3. We are told that we need to be encouraging our Christian brothers and sisters. Try and think of someone you know who may be struggling in his or her faith, or that you feel needs encouragement. Ask God to bring someone to mind. Send them a card, note, or e-mail to encourage them.

Day 6 — 1 Peter 3:18-22

Note: Noah was saved through faith in almighty God. He came through the water, which destroyed the rest of mankind.

Q: In what way does water "save us"? (v. 21)

Something to think about:

When Christians talk about being "saved" they mean that God in his mercy has saved them from the punishment that sin deserves—hell. Noah warned the people about God's impending judgment but they didn't take any notice and they carried on living in sin until God sent the flood. In the twenty-first century we suffer the same problem. People do not take the message of judgment seriously. But one day Jesus is coming back to judge the earth. Pray for unbelievers that God would have mercy on them and save them from His coming judgment.

Day 7 Psalm 119:9-11; Psalm 1

Note: An unknown writer said this of the Bible, "This Book is the mind of God on the state of man, the way of salvation, the doom of sinners, and the happiness of believers. Its doctrines are holy, its precepts (laws for how we are to live) are binding; its histories are true, and its decisions are immutable. Read it to be wise, believe it to be safe, practice it to be holy. It contains light to direct you, food to support you, and comfort to cheer you. It is the traveler's map, the pilgrim's staff, the pilot's compass, the soldier's sword, and the Christian's charter. Here paradise is restored, heaven opened, and the gates of hell disclosed. Christ is its grand subject, our good its design, and the glory of God its end. It should fill the memory, rule the heart, and guide the feet. Read it slowly, frequently, prayerfully. It is a mine of wealth, a paradise of glory, and a river of pleasure. Follow its precepts and it will lead you to Calvary, to the empty tomb, to a resurrected life in Christ; yes, to glory itself, for eternity."

Q: How does a Christian keep his or her life pleasing to God? (Ps. 119:10)

Q: According to Psalm 1, how often should we be reading the Bible?

Day 7 continued overleaf...

Day 7 continued ...

Something to think about:

As you work your way through the Bible write down any questions you may have and give them to your youth leader or pastor. Do not be afraid to ask difficult questions about your faith and about the Scriptures. They have stood up to 2000 years of intense criticism and scrutiny so the likelihood is that your question(s) will have been asked before.

Appendix

Coping With Temptation

"No one can be caught in a place he does not visit." (Anon)

Read James 1:13-16

The first thing we need to know about temptation is that it is not a sin to be tempted, it only becomes a sin when we give in to temptation and so fall into sin. There are various steps we can take that will help us as we fight temptation in its various forms every day of our lives.

1. We need to be continually renewing our minds, and we do this by daily reading and digesting the Word of God in accordance with Romans 12:1-2.

2. We need to know what God expects from his children.

What God does expect

1. We must be clear that God demands perfection from us. In Matthew 5:48 Christ set us the highest ideal of how we are to love when he told us to "be perfect, therefore, as you heavenly Father is perfect". In 1 John the apostle John wrote to the church "so that you would not sin". He is even more explicit in 1 John 3:6 when he says, "No one who lives in him [Christ] keeps on sinning. No one who continues to sin has either seen him or known him." According to John those who claim to know God cannot "walk in the darkness" (1 Jn. 1:6).

   Yet John also says, "if we claim to be without sin, we deceive ourselves and the truth is not in us ... If we claim we have not sinned, we make him out to be a liar and his word has no place in our lives" (1 Jn. 1:8-10). How are to make sense of these two seemingly contradictory statements?

   We need to be clear that we will never be able to achieve any kind of "sinless perfection" in our earthly lives. God knows that we will never attain such perfection in this life. Romans 7:7-25 is evidence of this. As we read this passage it is apparent that even the apostle Paul struggled with his sinful nature. "I know that nothing good lives in me, that is, in my sinful nature. For I have the desire to do what is good, but I cannot carry it out. For what I do is not the good I want to do; no, the evil I do not want to do—this I keep on doing" (Rom. 7:18-19).

However, the inevitability of sin does not give us a license to indulge in it. Paul is clear earlier in the letter to the Romans: "Shall we go on sinning, so that grace may increase? By no means!" (Rom. 6:1). Thus, God demands perfection from us but there is no way we can meet that demand. That is the tension of the Christian walk. We cannot claim sinlessness yet neither can we live our lives as though sin does not matter. Therefore, our task as believers is to daily put to death our old sinful nature and offer our bodies as "slaves to righteousness" (Rom. 6:18). We are to grow more and more "Christ like" and strive for the holiness that God demands from us.

2. God expects us to keep short accounts. In other words when you sin against God and against your fellow believer repent as soon as possible and move on.

3. Live in the present and not in the past. Don't look back to past sins and past wrongs. Romans 8:33 should be an immense comfort for those of us who struggle in this area. "Who will bring any charge against those whom God has chosen? It is God who justifies." In other words, God has declared us not guilty of all our sins: past, present, and future.

4. He wants you to grow in grace and knowledge of Jesus (2 Pet. 3:18).

5. He wants you to actively resist temptation—it is a matter of yielding your will to God.

What God does not expect

He does not expect you to set unrealistic goals for yourself. For example, never looking at another person of the opposite sex again, or moving to a deserted island to escape your sins! It is not wrong to have high moral ambitions as long as you're realistic when it comes to achieving them. Remember that you are a sinner. Somebody once said that "we must not persist with perfection or nothing, or we'll end up with nothing."

Know your enemy

When we know our enemy we can find his weaknesses. Satan has many guises. He can appear as:

"An angel of light to try to lead God's people astray" (2 Cor. 11:14).

"A roaring lion trying to devour the children of God" (1 Pet. 5:8-9).

Thus, to fend off the devil we need to be continually renewing our minds with the Word of God. As long as you are walking with the Lord you have nothing to fear from Satan.

Know your own limitations

This is key in your fight with the enemy. What are the weakest areas in your life: anger, gossip, laziness, pride, sex? This is where the devil usually attacks us. Pray to God for the strength to overcome your weaknesses.

Walk closely with the Lord

Daily contact with the Lord is of paramount importance. You need to fix your eyes upon Jesus. When you are focused on him and on his Word then your mind and will are less likely to wander.

Be self-disciplined

"Flee the evil desires of youth, and pursue righteousness, faith, love, and peace, along with those who call on the Lord, with a pure heart" (2 Tim. 2:22).

Remember: failure will happen

C.S. Lewis once said: "No amount of falls will really undo us if we keep picking ourselves up each time." We are a fallen people and we sin every day of our lives yet God loves us despite our weaknesses. He knew us before we were born, he knows the number of hairs on our head, and he is always on hand to forgive us when we slip up. God, speaking through the prophet Isaiah, promises us: "I, even I, am he who blots out your transgressions, for my own sake, and remembers your sins no more" (Is. 43:25).

Preparing for
BAPTISM
A Personal Diary
Mez McConnell